January
Patterns & Projects

Newbridge Educational Publishing, LLC
New York

The purchase of this book entitles the buyer to duplicate
these pages for use by students in the buyer's classroom.
All other permissions must be obtained from the publisher.

ISBN: 1-58273-129-2

Photo Credit: (cover and title page) Randy Ury/The Stock Market

Table of Contents

January Classroom Calendar **5**
It's About Time 8
Set the Clock 10
"My Daily Planner" Books 11

Months of the Year File-Folder Game **12**
New Year's Hats and Sashes 16
Unscramble the Calendar 18
Months of the Year Poem 19

Happy New Year Cards **20**
New Year's Rhymes 24
Making "Cents" in the New Year 25
Recommended Reading 26

The Life of Martin Luther King, Jr. **27**
I Have a Dream 28
Martin Luther King, Jr. Book 29
Recommended Reading 33

The Chinese New Year **34**
Chinese New Year Dragon Costume 35
Chinese New Year Calendar 39
Calendar Hat 39

Chinese New Year Mobile **41**
Chinese New Year File-Folder Game. 45
Animal Categories 50
Go Fish 51
Chinese Food Party 52
Stir-Fried Noodles 53
Recommended Reading 54
Chinese Jump Rope 54

Winter Awards **55**
You're the Best! Badges 59
In Honor Of… 60

Winter Wonderland Doorknob Decorations **61**
Winter Wonderland Books 65
Shhh…It's Silent! 66
Finish the Winter Scene 67
Build an Igloo File-Folder Game. 68
Counting Cards 73

Table of Contents (continued)

Winter Weather Wheel **74**
The North Wind and the Sun—A Fable 78
The North Wind and the Sun Class Play 79
Weather Chart 80
Recommended Reading 80

JANUARY CLASSROOM CALENDAR

You need:
- large oaktag sheets
- crayons or markers
- scissors
- glue

1. Reproduce the January calendar on pages 6 and 7 once for each child. Have children color, mount on large sheets of oaktag, and cut out.
2. Help children determine which day of the week January will begin on, and tell them to write a number 1 in the top right corner of the box for that day. Then let children fill in the remaining days with numbers 2 through 31.
3. Talk about special days that will occur during the month of January. Children can indicate those days on their calendar with writing or pictures. Some dates to note include:
   January 1: New Year's Day
   January 15: Martin Luther King's birthday
4. Other dates that may be entered on the calendar include classmates' birthdays, class field trips, classroom guests, or special assemblies.
5. Children can take their calendars home and hang them on their bedroom wall.

January Classroom Calendar Pattern

JANU

SUNDAY	MONDAY	TUESDAY	WEDNE

JARY

...SDAY	THURSDAY	FRIDAY	SATURDAY

IT'S ABOUT TIME

You need:
• crayons or markers
• brass fasteners

1. Reproduce the clock, hour hand, and minute hand patterns on page 9 once for each daily class activity. Have volunteers color and cut out.
2. Help children attach the hour and minute hands to the clock with a brass paper fastener, as shown, so the hands are movable.
3. The teacher writes the appropriate activity on the clock face (gym, lunch, art, playtime, dismissal, etc.), arranges the clocks in chronological order to show the day's events, and places them in a visible place in the classroom. It is simple to rearrange the clock order and times or add a new clock face to reflect schedule changes during each week.

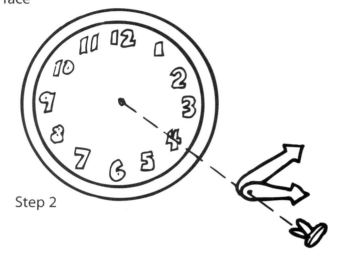

Step 2

Clock and Hands Patterns

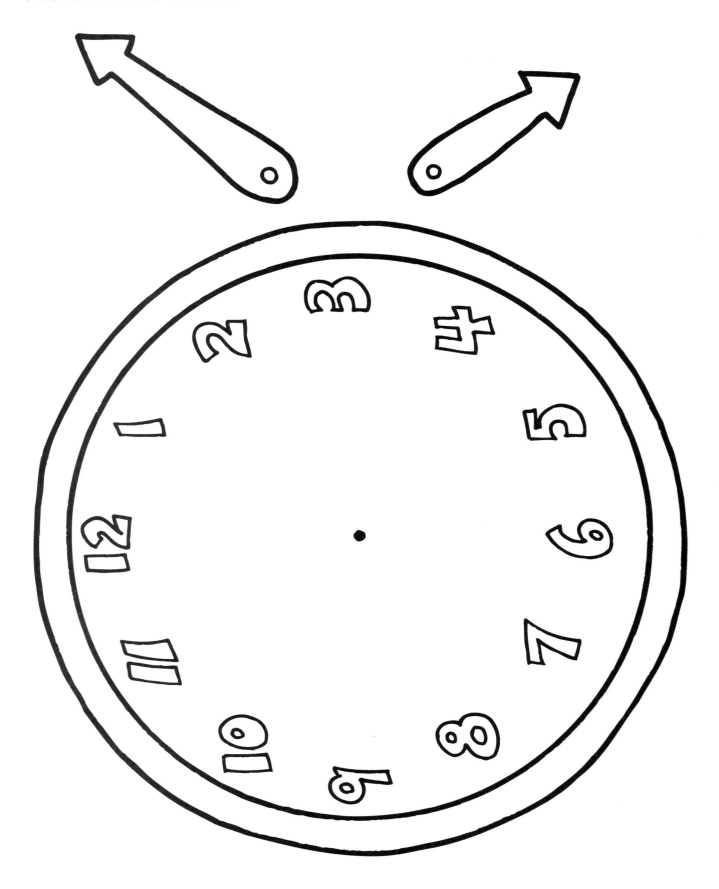

SET THE CLOCK

You need:
• crayons or markers
• oaktag
• glue
• scissors
• brass fasteners

1. Reproduce the clock, hour hand, and minute hand patterns on page 9 once for each child. Have children color, mount on oaktag, and cut out.
2. Help children attach the hour and minute hands to the clock with a brass paper fastener, as shown, so the hands are movable.
3. Have children set their clocks to various times that you announce, such as 3:00 or 9:30.
4. Invite volunteers to set their clocks to a time they choose. Let them show the clock to classmates, who then identify the time that is indicated.

Step 2

"MY DAILY PLANNER" BOOKS

You need:
• drawing paper (several sheets for each child)
• crayons or markers
• stapler

Children can make daily planners that show the things they do each day. Follow these steps.

1. Ask children each to think about the things they do at different times during the day, such as eating breakfast, going to school, or playing games at home.
2. Invite children to draw several pictures on individual sheets of paper showing the activities they do during the day. Help children label each picture with the time of day, such as "8:30 a.m." Children can write or dictate a caption for each picture, such as, "At 8:30 in the morning I get on the school bus."
3. When all the pictures are complete, help children put their drawings in their proper time sequence.
4. Let children draw a cover for their book and write the title "My Daily Planner." Staple all the pages together.
5. Encourage children to share their books with classmates to discover how their daily schedules are similar or different.

MONTHS OF THE YEAR FILE-FOLDER GAME

HOW TO MAKE

You need:
• crayons or markers
• glue
• letter-sized file folder
• clear contact paper
• scissors
• rubber bands
• envelope

1. Reproduce the game board on pages 14 and 15 three times. Color each set and glue one game board to the inside of a letter-sized file folder.
2. Reproduce the "How to Play" instructions on page 13 and glue to the front of the file folder.
3. Laminate the other game boards. Cut apart the months to make two sets of game cards.
4. Wrap a rubber band around each set of game cards. Store the cards in an envelope glued to the back of the folder.

MONTHS OF THE YEAR FILE-FOLDER GAME

HOW TO PLAY
(for 2 players)

1. Each child takes one set of game cards, shuffles them, and places them facedown in two horizontal rows.
2. One child goes first and turns over one of his or her own cards, and one of the other player's cards. If the two cards match, that player places one of the cards in the matching space on the game board and places the other card faceup in a pile next to him or her. The player's turn continues for as long as he or she is able to match two cards.
3. If the player does not get a match, he or she places the cards facedown in the same spots and the next player goes.
4. Play continues until all the matching spaces on the game board are filled. The player with the most faceup cards is the winner.

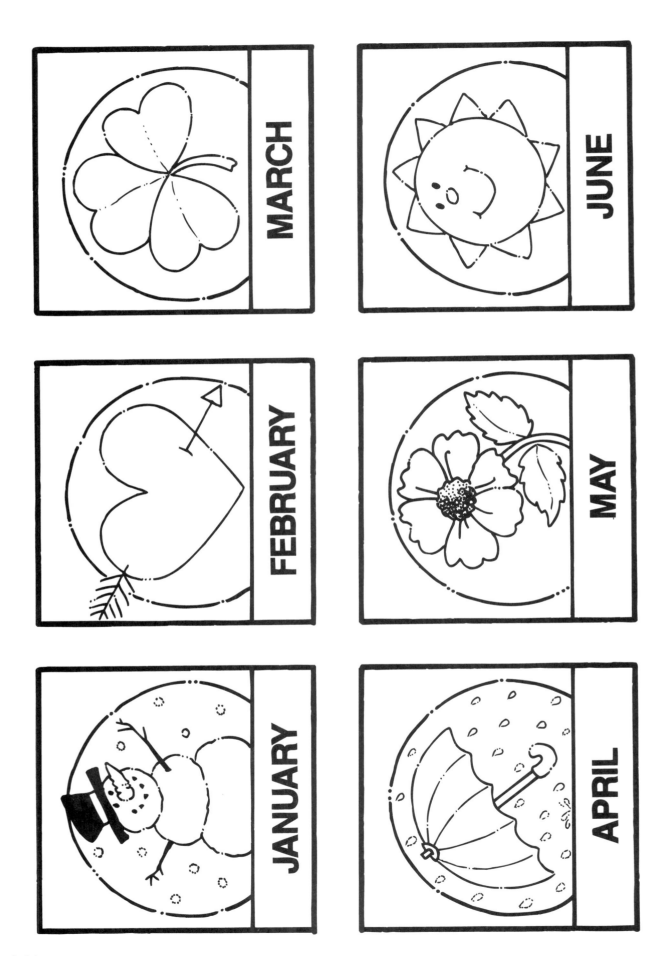

MARCH

JUNE

FEBRUARY

MAY

JANUARY

APRIL

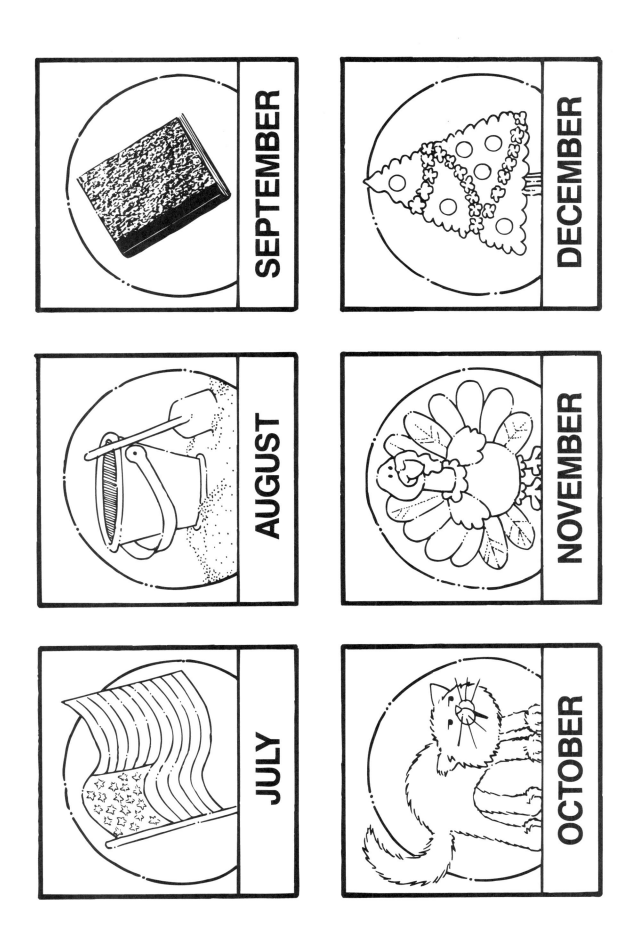

SEPTEMBER

DECEMBER

AUGUST

NOVEMBER

JULY

OCTOBER

NEW YEAR'S HATS AND SASHES

You need:
• crayons or markers
• stapler
• hole puncher
• yarn
• 6" x 24" strips of construction paper

1. Reproduce the New Year's hat pattern on page 17 once for each child. Have children color the hats.
2. Help each child form the hat into a cone shape. Holding the page horizontally with the cat facing out, roll the paper so the top right corner aligns with the corner formed by the printed stars. Staple the hat where indicated.
3. Punch a hole on both sides of the hat, as shown. Thread a piece of yarn through both holes and tie the hat onto each child's head.
4. To make the sashes, trim the ends of two 6" x 24" strips of construction paper at an angle, as shown. Staple together at both ends. Make 12 sashes, writing a different month of the year on each sash.
5. For activities, see Months of the Year Poem on page 19.

Step 2

Step 3

Step 4

New Year's Hat Pattern

STAPLE HERE

HAPPY NEW YEAR

UNSCRAMBLE THE CALENDAR

Name _____

Robbie Rabbit has mixed up the order of the months below.
On the lines provided, write the correct order.

#	Month	#	Month
1	JUNE	7	
	SEPTEMBER		
2	MAY	8	
3	FEBRUARY	9	
	DECEMBER		
4	JANUARY	10	
	JULY		
5	OCTOBER	11	
	MARCH		
6	NOVEMBER	12	
	AUGUST		
	APRIL		

18

Newbridge

MONTHS OF THE YEAR POEM

Ask children to wear their New Year's hats. Choose 12 children to wear the sashes and be the "months." Have each month, starting with January, come to the front of the room and recite his or her verse. (You may want to choose children according to the months of their birthdays.) Repeat until all the children in the class have had a turn.

The new year begins,
The cold winds blow.
In January
We play in the snow.

In February
Folks celebrate
Two presidents
We think were great.

Then winter ends as
We March into spring,
Wondering what the
New season will bring.

The birds start to sing.
Watch nature's powers
As we walk through the park
In April showers.

Beautiful flowers
Are blooming in May.
And hats off to Mom
On her special day!

Dad gets his turn in
The middle of June.
School's almost over.
Vacation is soon!

Picnics and ball games,
See the flags flying high.
Have a wonderful time.
Happy Fourth of July!

August is time for
Long days at the beach.
We swing on the swings
Way up out of reach.

Then, quick, hurry up—
One last splash in the pool!
Here comes September.
We'll soon be in school.

Witches and goblins
And ghosts gather near
Late in October—
Halloween's here!

November's no time
For trick-or-treat pranks.
Instead gather round
And let us give thanks.

December comes last,
A great end to the year,
With parties and laughter
And holiday cheer!

HAPPY NEW YEAR CARDS

You need:
- crayons or markers
- scissors
- construction paper
- tape
- glitter, ribbons, colored tissue paper
- glue

1. Let children each choose a pattern on pages 21 through 23 to use for a holiday card. Reproduce one pattern for each child. Have children color the pattern and cut out.
2. Give each child two sheets of colored construction paper. Tell children to place the two sheets side by side and attach them with tape along the middle, as shown.
3. Have children fold their paper pages to form a greeting card. Have them glue their pattern to the front of the card.
4. Children may further decorate their New Year's cards with glitter, ribbon, colored tissue paper, or other decorative materials.

Step 2

Happy New Year Card Pattern

NEW YEAR'S RHYMES

Invite children to brainstorm a list of words they associate with New Year's. Record their responses on the board or on chart paper. After the list is complete, challenge children to think of words that rhyme with each response. Add the rhyming words to your list, as shown in the chart below.

new	year	snow	hat	noise	fun
true	cheer	know	cat	boys	sun
you	near	show	that	toys	won
too	here	slow	fat	joys	begun
blue	dear	go	sat	enjoys	run

Now encourage small groups of children to work together to write New Year's poems to include in their greeting cards. Tell them to use the rhyming words from the list as possible rhymes in their poems. Give these examples:

Hooray! It is a brand-new year!
Everyone is full of good cheer!

There are lots of people having fun.
The new year has only just begun.

MAKING "CENTS" IN THE NEW YEAR

You need:
- empty coffee cans
- crayons or markers
- scissors
- colored tissue paper
- tape
- glue

1. Talk with children about the idea of New Year's resolutions. Explain that a New Year's resolution is a kind of promise that people make at the beginning of the year to try to improve themselves in some way.
2. Invite children to think of New Year's resolutions they would like to make, such as, "I will help my friends in class" or "I will make my bed each day at home." Let children share their resolutions with the class.
3. Inform children that they can make another special New Year's resolution: to make "cents" in the classroom! How is that done? Ask children to save pennies they earn or find throughout the year. They can keep their pennies in a bank made from an empty coffee can.
4. To make their banks, let children wrap and tape colored tissue paper around the outside of the coffee can. Then have them color and cut out one of the three patterns on pages 21 through 23. Finally, have them glue the pattern to the front of the can.
5. At the end of the year, have children empty their penny banks and count how much money they have saved. They might use the money for any number of things: to donate to a community nonprofit organization, to contribute as part of a class field trip, or to sponsor a class party, for example.

RECOMMENDED READING

Read some of the following books about New Year's to the class. Place the books on a reading table or in a bookcase so children may look at them during their free time.

Goodbye Old Year, Hello New Year by Frank Modell, published by Greenwillow.
Griselda's New Year by Marjorie Weinman Sharmat, published by Macmillan.
Happy New Year by Emily Kelley, published by Carolrhoda Books.
Happy New Year, Charlie Brown by Charles M. Schultz, published by Random House.
Miss Flora McFlimsy and the Baby New Year by Mariana, published by Lothrop, Lee & Shepard.
New Year's Day by Aliki, published by Crowell.
The New Year's Mystery by Joan Lowery Nixon, published by A. Whitman.
New Year's Poems selected by Myra Cohn Livingston, published by Holiday House.
New Year's by Nancy Reese, published by Aro.
Un-Happy New Year, Emma! by James Stevenson, published by Greenwillow.

THE LIFE OF MARTIN LUTHER KING, JR.

Share the following information about Martin Luther King, Jr. with the class. Then discuss the questions that come after.

Martin Luther King, Jr. was born in Atlanta, Georgia, on January 15, 1929. Martin's father was a minister. His mother was a schoolteacher. Martin had a big sister named Christine and a younger brother named Alfred.

Martin was a smart and popular child. He had many friends in his neighborhood, some black and some white. Martin loved to play ball with them. He never got into a fight. Martin didn't like to fight.

When Martin was a child, black people were not treated the same as white people in the South. Laws prohibited blacks from using the same playgrounds, restaurants, water fountains, and schools as whites. After a while, Martin's white friends stopped playing with him. That made Martin sad and angry.

"When I grow up, I will change the law," Martin said. He worked hard in school. He even skipped two grades. Later, Martin went on to college.

After college, Martin became a minister. In 1953, he married Coretta Scott. They moved to Montgomery, Alabama, where Martin was head of a church.

One day in 1955, something happened in Montgomery that changed the life of Martin Luther King, Jr. and everyone else there. A woman named Rosa Parks refused to give up her bus seat for a white person, even though it was the law. Rosa Parks felt the law was unfair. She was arrested.

Martin thought the law was unfair, too. He led a protest. No black people rode the buses in Montgomery for a whole year. Finally, the law was changed and blacks and whites were allowed to sit together on the same buses.

Martin believed that other laws could be changed, too. He led peaceful marches and gave many speeches. He said, "I have a dream." It was a dream of freedom for all people.

Martin's hard work paid off. In 1964, a law was passed for the whole country. It said that all people could share everything—parks, restaurants, schools.

Martin Luther King, Jr. became famous. He won many prizes and awards for his work. But some people did not like what Martin Luther King had done. In 1968, a man shot and killed Martin in Memphis, Tennessee.

Although Martin Luther King, Jr. died, his dream of peace and freedom lives on. Today, we celebrate his birthday as a national holiday on January 15.

1. Why do you think it is important to remember Dr. King?
2. What are some good ways to celebrate Martin Luther King Day?
3. What are some words you can think of to describe what Dr. King did (e.g., *brave, hard*, etc.)?

Social Studies/Social Awareness/Writing/Drawing

I HAVE A DREAM

Explain to children that Martin Luther King, Jr. gave a famous speech in our nation's capital, Washington, D.C., in 1963. Thousands of people gathered at the Lincoln Memorial to hear Dr. King. In his speech, he told about a dream he had—he wished that people of all races and religions would one day live together in peace.

Invite children to think about something good that they would like to happen. It might be a dream for themselves, for their family, for their friends, or for people all over the world. Ask children to write several sentences that describe their dream. Also invite them to draw a picture to go with their writing.

Later, have children tape their page of writing and artwork to the blank sheet of construction paper that is the third page of their Martin Luther King, Jr. book (see page 29).

MARTIN LUTHER KING, JR. BOOK

You need:
• crayons or markers
• scissors
• construction paper
• glue
• stapler

1. Reproduce all the patterns on pages 30 through 32 once for each child.
2. Have children color and cut out each pattern. Have them mount each pattern on a separate sheet of construction paper.
3. Provide one additional sheet of construction paper for each child.
4. Have children arrange and stack the sheets so that the picture of Martin Luther King, Jr. is the cover, the "I Have a Dream" banner comes second, the children holding hands in a circle comes third, and the additional sheet comes fourth.
5. Staple each child's four pages together to create a book.

Children Holding Hands Pattern

RECOMMENDED READING

Read some of the following books about Martin Luther King, Jr. to the class. Place the books on a reading table or in a bookcase so children may look at them during their free time.

Martin Luther King Day by Linda Lowery, published by Carolrhoda Books.

Martin Luther King, Jr.: A Biography for Young Children by Carol Hilgartner Schlank and Barbara Metzger, published by Gryphon House.

Martin Luther King, Jr.: A Man Who Changed Things by Carol Greene, published by Children's Press.

Martin Luther King, Jr.: A Picture Story by Margaret Boone-Jones, published by Children's Press.

Martin Luther King, Jr. Day by Dianne MacMillan, published by Enslow Publishers.

Martin Luther King, Jr.: Free At Last by David Adler, published by Holiday House.

A Picture Book of Martin Luther King, Jr. by David Adler, published by Holiday House.

THE CHINESE NEW YEAR

Have a class discussion about the Chinese New Year. Explain to children that people in China celebrate the coming of the New Year between January 10 and February 19, depending upon when the moon appears in the sky. Tell children that Chinese New Year is a very important holiday and has been celebrated for a great many years. For the New Year, people clean their homes and then decorate them. They make and hang beautiful paper chains.

Let children know that when Chinese New Year is celebrated, there are wonderful parades led by people wearing dragon costumes. Dragons are a symbol for good luck in China. Sometimes firecrackers are set off. Children enjoy flying kites at this time.

Red is the color for good luck in China, and many presents wrapped in red paper are given to friends and family. Lots of decorations are also colored red.

The animals shown in the Chinese New Year Mobile on page 41 are Chinese symbols for different years. Each year is named for one of the twelve animals. Discuss with children what kinds of characteristics each animal has.

Ask children to think about some things that are the same about the way Americans celebrate the New Year and the way Chinese people celebrate the New Year. Then ask volunteers to describe some of the differences.

CHINESE NEW YEAR DRAGON COSTUME

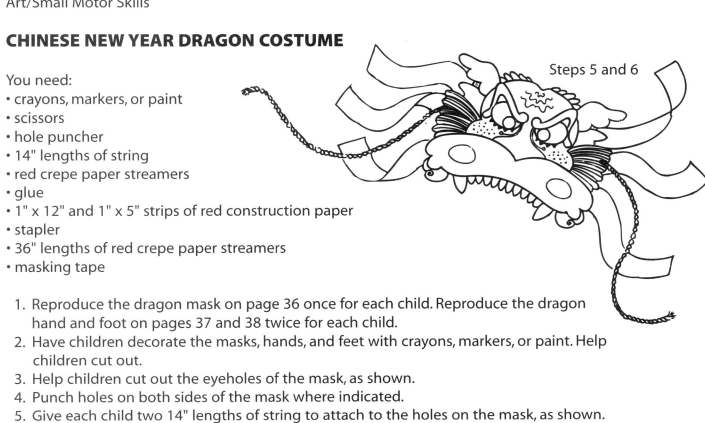

Steps 5 and 6

You need:
• crayons, markers, or paint
• scissors
• hole puncher
• 14" lengths of string
• red crepe paper streamers
• glue
• 1" x 12" and 1" x 5" strips of red construction paper
• stapler
• 36" lengths of red crepe paper streamers
• masking tape

1. Reproduce the dragon mask on page 36 once for each child. Reproduce the dragon hand and foot on pages 37 and 38 twice for each child.
2. Have children decorate the masks, hands, and feet with crayons, markers, or paint. Help children cut out.
3. Help children cut out the eyeholes of the mask, as shown.
4. Punch holes on both sides of the mask where indicated.
5. Give each child two 14" lengths of string to attach to the holes on the mask, as shown.
6. Have children cut red crepe paper strips about 2" x 4" long and glue them to the sides of the mask, as shown.
7. Help children fold down the flaps on the dragon hands and feet along the dotted lines. Then give each child two 1" x 12" strips of red construction paper. Help children staple the strips to each side of the dragon feet, forming loops that the children can slip their own ankles through, as shown.
8. Give each child two 1" x 5" strips of red construction paper. Have children staple the strips to the backs of the dragon hands, forming loops to slip their hands through, as shown.
9. Have each child cut out the triangle pattern on page 37 and trace it six times onto red construction paper.
10. Help each child cut out the triangles and glue them along the edge of a 36" crepe paper streamer, as shown. Attach the streamers to children's backs with masking tape.
11. Encourage children to dress up in their dragon costumes and form a parade. If possible, obtain a recording of some Chinese music to play during the parade.

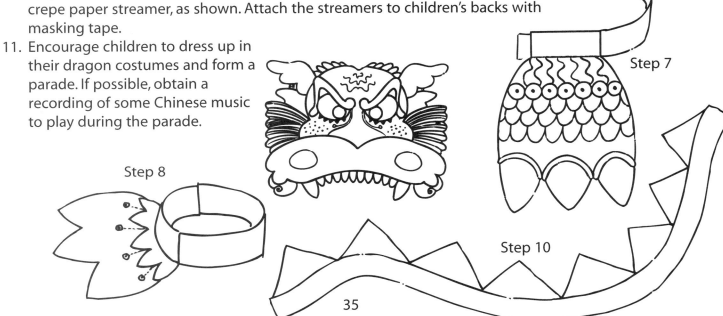

Step 8

Step 7

Step 10

Dragon Mask Pattern

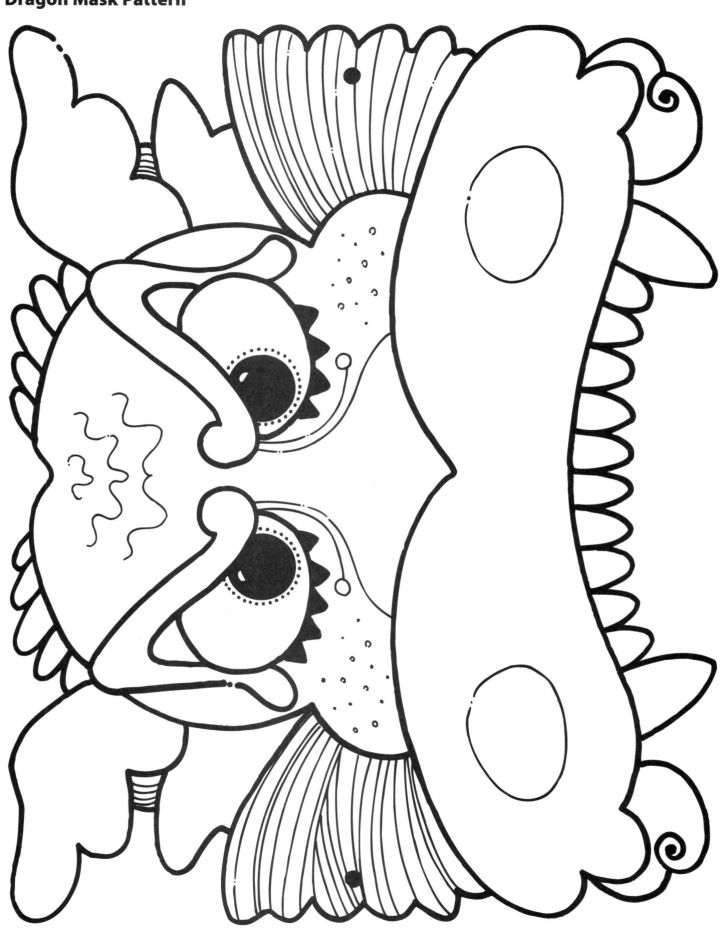

Dragon Hand and Triangle Pattern

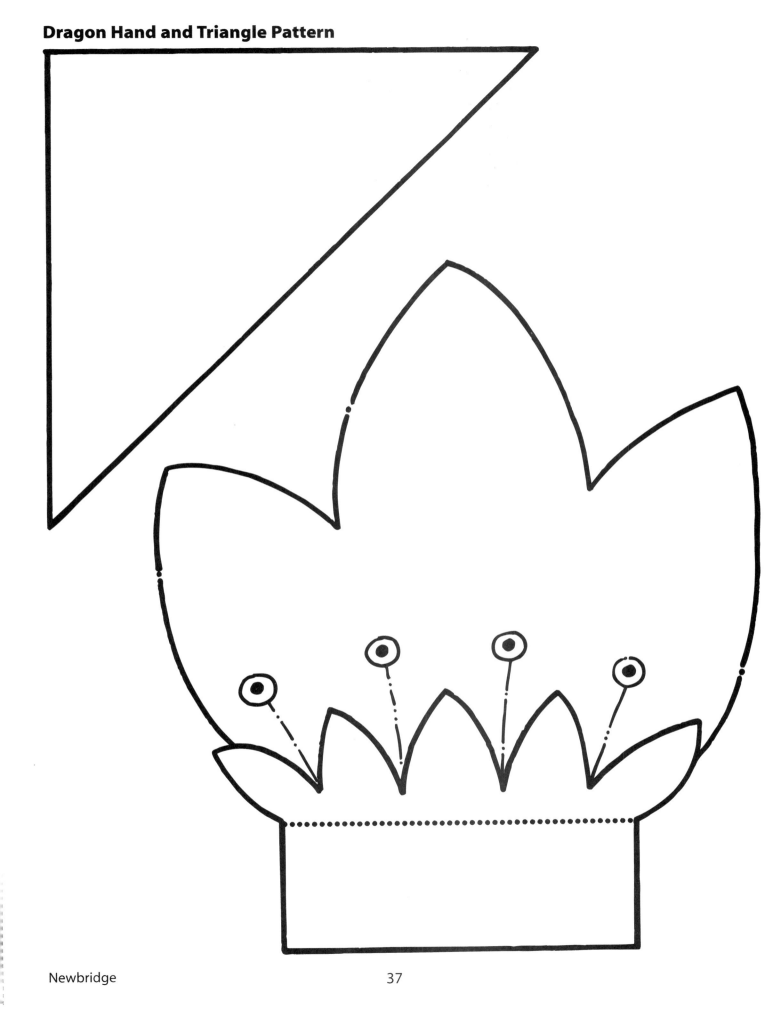

Dragon Foot Pattern

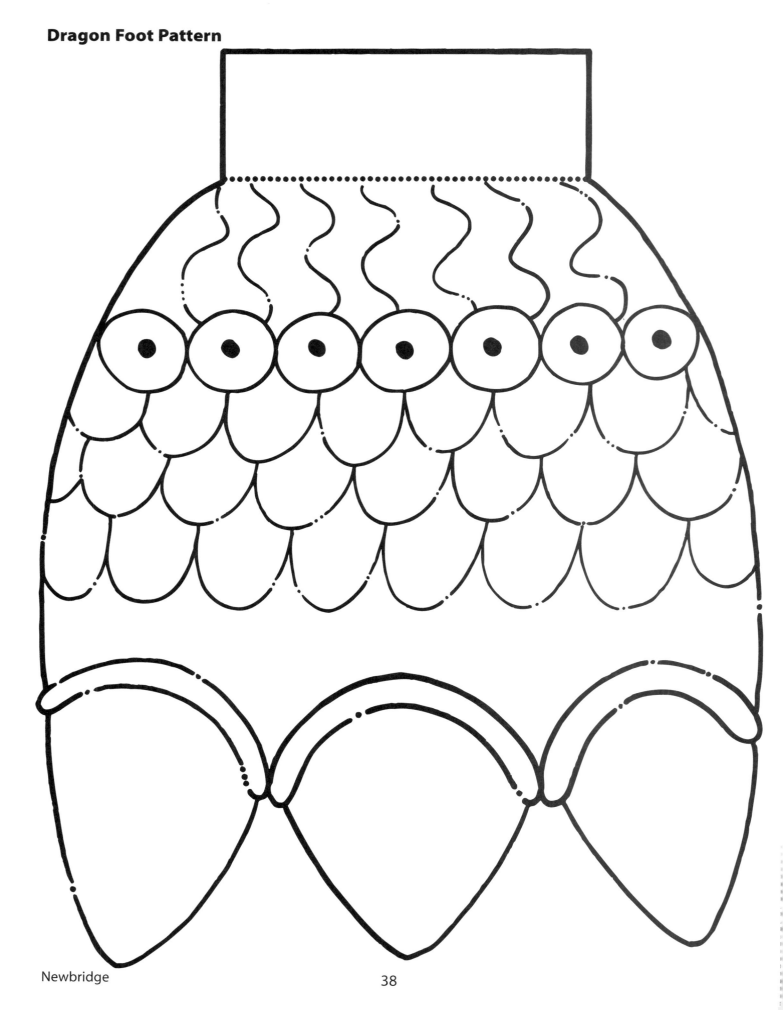

CHINESE NEW YEAR CALENDAR

Chinese New Year is celebrated between January 10 and February 19 each year. It is celebrated at a different time than the traditional New Year on January 1 because the Chinese calendar is different from ours. The Chinese calendar operates on a 12-year cycle. Each of the 12 years in the cycle is named for a different animal. Chinese people believe that people born during a particular animal's year are said to have certain characteristics in common with that animal. (Chinese numbers and letters look different from ours, too!)

CALENDAR HAT

You need:
• crayons or markers
• scissors
• 33 1/3-rpm record
• large butcher paper or newsprint
• stapler
• 10" lengths of string

1. Reproduce one calendar on page 40 for each child. Have children color and cut out.
2. Trace around the edge of an old 33 1/3-rpm record onto large pieces of butcher paper or newsprint once for each child. Mark the center of the circle through the hole in the middle of the record.
3. Have each child cut out the circle and cut a slit about 6" long into the center of the circle, as shown.
4. Show children how to overlap the edges of the slit, forming a point in the center of the circle, as shown. Staple in place.
5. Staple two 10" lengths of string on opposite sides of the circle.
6. Glue the calendar to the hat, as shown.
7. Ask children questions about the Chinese calendar. For example, what is the name of the animal for this year? Ask children to describe this year's animal. Have volunteers tell the class which animal is their favorite and why. Help children figure out which animals represent the years they were born. What characteristics do those animals have?

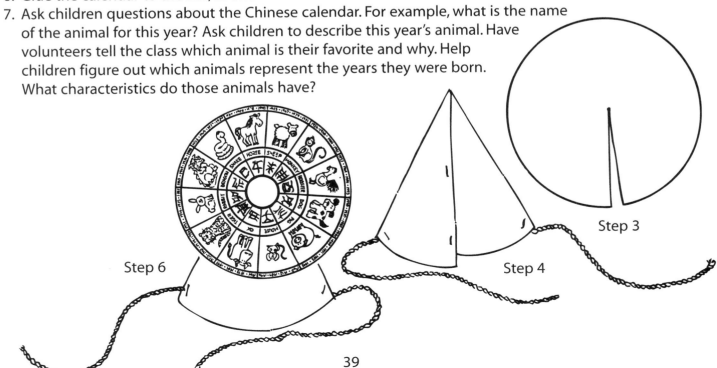

Step 6

Step 4

Step 3

CHINESE NEW YEAR MOBILE

You need:
• crayons or markers
• glue
• oaktag
• scissors
• hole puncher
• string
• stapler

1. Reproduce all the Chinese New Year patterns on pages 42 through 44 once for each child. Have children color, mount on oaktag, and cut out.
2. Help each child punch a hole near the top of each figure and thread a length of string through the hole.
3. Give each child a 4" x 24" strip of oaktag. Help each child label the strip "Chinese New Year."
4. Help each child punch four holes along the top of each strip and twelve holes along the bottom of each strip, as shown.
5. Show children how to thread the Chinese New Year figures through the bottom holes, as shown.
6. Have children staple the oaktag strips in a circle.
7. Help each child thread string through the four holes on the top of the strip and tie together, as shown.
8. Hang the mobiles from the ceiling during Chinese New Year.

Steps 4 and 5

Step 7

CHINESE NEW YEAR FILE-FOLDER GAME

HOW TO MAKE

You need:
- crayons or markers
- glue
- letter-sized file folder
- clear contact paper
- brass fastener
- scissors

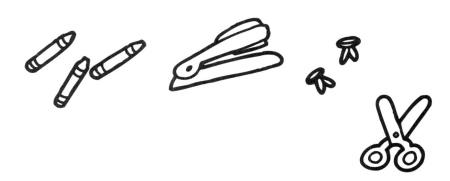

1. Reproduce the game board on pages 48 and 49, the "How to Play" instructions on page 46, and the spinner on page 47 once. Reproduce the game cards on page 47 once for each player.
2. Have children color the game board, game cards, and spinner.
3. Glue the game board to the inside of a letter-sized file folder.
4. Glue the instructions to the front of the file folder. Laminate.
5. Have children cut out the game cards.
6. Ask a volunteer to assemble the spinner, using a brass fastener to attach the arrow, as shown.

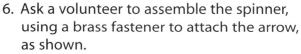

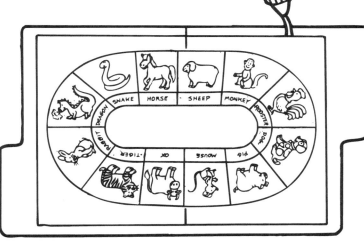

CHINESE NEW YEAR FILE-FOLDER GAME

HOW TO PLAY
(for 2 to 4 players)

1. Each player receives a deck of 12 animal cards. Players go in alphabetical order according to their first names.
2. The first player spins, then takes one of his or her animal cards that begins with the letter on the spinner and places it faceup on the matching space on the game board. For example, after spinning a *D*, the player may place a dog or a dragon on the board.
3. If a letter is spun that does not match any animal card (*F*, for example), the player does nothing, and the next player spins.
4. All players continue to take turns spinning, following the same procedure.
5. The first player to get all 12 animal cards on the game board wins.

Chinese New Year Game Cards and Spinner Patterns

SNAKE

HORSE

DRAGON

RABBIT

TIGER

OX

SHEEP

MONKEY

ROOSTER

DOG

PIG

MOUSE

ANIMAL CATEGORIES

The Chinese calendar contains 12 animals. Have children find magazine pictures of the animals, or supply pictures from books. Then organize the children into groups. Let each group categorize the animals in a different way. Categories might be based on the following:

Which animals have four feet? Which have two feet? Which have no feet?

Which animals have a long tail? Which have a short tail?

Which animals can fly? Which animals cannot fly?

Which animals move quickly? Which animals move slowly?

Which animals do people keep as pets? Which animals are not pets?

Which animals give us food? Which animals do not give us food?

Which animals are raised on a farm? Which are not raised on a farm?

After all groups have categorized their pictures, invite each group to display and explain its categories to the rest of the class.

GO FISH

Children can use the animal pattern cards on page 47 to play a card game similar to "Go Fish." This game may be played in groups of four.

1. Each player puts his or her 12 cards together with everyone else's in the group. Shuffle them to make one big deck.
2. A dealer gives four cards, facedown, to each player. The other cards are left in a pile in the middle.
3. Players look at their cards. The dealer goes first. The dealer asks another player for a card that matches one of his or her own. For example, the dealer says, "Melissa, do you have any roosters?"
4. If Melissa has any roosters, she must hand them over to the dealer. Then the dealer can ask for another type of card from another player.
5. If Melissa has no roosters, she says, "Go Fish," and the dealer must pick from the pile.
6. A second player then gets to ask for a card. Play follows the same procedure as before.
7. When a player collects all four cards of a particular animal (e.g., four roosters), the player sets them aside and announces, "I have a book of roosters."
8. The game ends when all cards have been collected into books. The player with the most books wins.

CHINESE FOOD PARTY

Part of the Chinese New Year celebration is a festive meal. Talk with your children about traditional Chinese foods. If possible, distribute Chinese restaurant menus and read the names of some of the dishes listed. Let children who have eaten any of these dishes describe them to the class.

Have your own festive classroom meal of popular (and simple) Chinese foods. Your menu might include:

fried noodles	mandarin oranges	rice
duck sauce	fortune cookies	kumquats
Chinese almond cookies	egg rolls	tea

Invite children to try each item on the menu. Then have them offer words to describe each taste. Record their responses on a chart similar to the one below.

MENU

FRIED NOODLES ——— SPICY
FORTUNE COOKIES ——— CRISPY
RICE ——————— PLAIN
EGG ROLLS ———— SPICY
TEA ————————— HOT
MANDARIN ORANGES— SWEET

STIR-FRIED NOODLES
(Serves 20 to 25)

Make the following recipe for your class. To allow children an authentic cultural experience, let them try to eat noodles with chopsticks. Attach a small rubber band around both chopsticks about 2" from the top. Show children how to hold the chopsticks like a pencil, inserting the middle finger between the chopsticks. (Children will enjoy trying to eat their noodles with the chopsticks, but be sure to provide forks or spoons as well.)

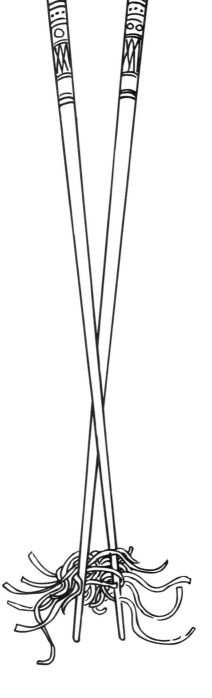

You need:
• 2 to 3 pounds Chinese noodles, vermicelli, or thin spaghetti
• large pot
• 4 carrots
• grater
• 1/4 to 1/2 cup vegetable or peanut oil
• electric skillet
• 1/4 cup soy sauce
• chopsticks
• forks or spoons
• paper plates
Optional: green peppers, celery

1. Cook the noodles in a large pot of boiling water until tender. Drain. Noodles can be cooked and chilled for convenience.
2. Ask children to wash the carrots. Then grate them. If desired, chop green peppers and celery into tiny pieces.
3. Heat the oil in the electric skillet.
4. Stir-fry the noodles about 5 minutes, adding the soy sauce and vegetables.
5. Spoon the noodles onto individual plates.

For dessert, give your class Chinese fortune cookies. Fortune cookies are available in many grocery stores. Explain to children what "fortune" is. Children will enjoy discovering the messages inside their cookies.

GOOD FORTUNE FOLLOWS THOSE WHO TEACH.

RECOMMENDED READING

Read some of the following books about China to your class. Place the books on a reading table or in a bookcase so that children may look at them during free time.

Big Bird in China by Jon Stone, published by Random House.
Friends Everywhere: A Visit to China by Mary Packard, published by Western Publishing.
Little Pear by Eleanor Lattimore, published by Harcourt Brace Jovanovich.
The Story About Ping by Marjorie Flack, published by Viking.
Tikki Tikki Tembo by Arlene Mosel, published by Henry Holt.

CHINESE JUMP ROPE

1. Take a piece of elastic 6' long and 1" wide. Sew the ends together to form a loop.
2. Have two children stand approximately 4' apart, facing each other. Slip the elastic over the children's ankles, as shown.
3. Show the rest of the class how to jump in and out of the space created inside the elastic band. Ask volunteers who have played Chinese jump rope to demonstrate their skills for the others.

WINTER AWARDS

You need:
- scissors
- crayons or markers
- glue
- glitter
- safety pins
- oaktag
- clay

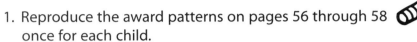
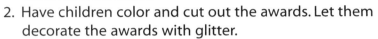

1. Reproduce the award patterns on pages 56 through 58 once for each child.
2. Have children color and cut out the awards. Let them decorate the awards with glitter.
3. Have children glue the trophy to oaktag and cut out. Then have them create a clay base for the award so it can stand by itself.

Winter Award Pattern

Winter Award Pattern

Winter Award Pattern

YOU'RE THE BEST! BADGES

You need:
- scissors
- crayons or markers
- glitter
- glue
- safety pins

1. Reproduce the badge pattern on page 58 once for each child.
2. Have children decorate the badges with crayons, markers, and glitter.
3. Fill in a badge for each child by using an area in which that child has excelled. For example, "Best Line Leader," "Terrific Snack Monitor," "Best Cleaner," and so on.
4. Hold an awards ceremony and pin the badges on the children as you announce their achievements to the class.

IN HONOR OF...

Have children hold an awards ceremony using the patterns they have designed
(see page 55). Follow these steps:

1. Ask each child to write his or her name on a slip of paper. Place all slips in a paper bag.
2. Have each child draw a slip from the bag. Tell children to prepare their certificate for the
   person whose name they drew. The certificate will be given in honor of something
   positive that child has done. For example:

   "Winter Award to Sue F. for being a good reader."

3. Hold a ceremony where children present their awards to the honorees. Have them read
   their certificates aloud as they present them. Also help them pin a badge on the honoree.
   In addition, children should present a trophy to the
   honoree. Create a "trophy case" in the classroom
   where all trophies can be displayed.

WINTER WONDERLAND DOORKNOB DECORATIONS

You need:
• oaktag
• crayons or markers
• scissors
• glue
• hole puncher

1. Let children each choose a pattern on pages 62 through 64 to use for their doorknob decoration. Reproduce the chosen pattern once for each child.
2. Have children color the pattern, mount on oaktag, and cut out.
3. Using a hole puncher, help children make a hole inside the circle near the top of the pattern. Then use scissors to cut around the entire circle and along the dotted line, as indicated on the pattern.
4. Children can fit the pattern decoration over their doorknob at the place where the hole has been made. Tell them to slip the oaktag on gently in order not to tear through the top of the pattern.

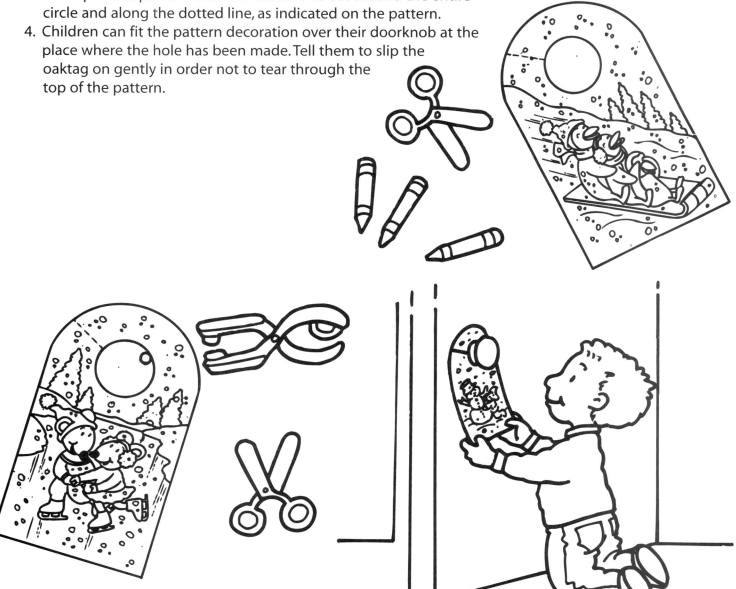

**Winter Wonderland
Doorknob Decoration
Pattern**

WINTER WONDERLAND BOOKS

You need:
• drawing paper
• construction paper
• crayons or markers
• scissors
• glue
• stapler

1. Distribute several sheets of drawing paper to each child.
2. Have children think about their favorite winter activities. Then ask them to draw a picture of each activity on a separate sheet of paper. Children may write or dictate a sentence that tells about each picture they have drawn. (For example: "In winter I like to go ice skating.")
3. Reproduce all three patterns on pages 62 through 64 once for each child. Help children cut out the characters.
4. Have children glue their characters on a sheet of construction paper to serve as the cover for their "Winter Wonderland Book." A second sheet of construction paper should be used as the backing for the book, after the last drawing.
5. Staple together all the pages of the "Winter Wonderland Book" for each child.

SHHH...IT'S SILENT!

Write the word *knob* on the board. Have children pronounce the word with you. Point out the letter *k* at the beginning of the word. Ask children if they hear the *k* sound when they say *knob*. (They do not.) Explain that some words in our language are spelled with a silent letter that is not heard when you say the word.

List the following words on the board:

knot	wrap	comb	sign
knit	write	climb	gnaw
know	wreck	crumb	assign

Say each word aloud with the children. Challenge the children to see who can identify the silent letter(s) that appears in each word.

Fill in the missing lines to complete the picture

Name _____

BUILD AN IGLOO FILE-FOLDER GAME

HOW TO MAKE

You need:
- crayons or markers
- glue
- oaktag
- scissors
- letter-sized file folder
- clear contact paper

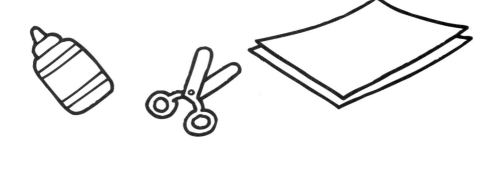

1. Reproduce the game board and "How to Play" instructions on pages 69 through 71 once for each pair of players. Reproduce the game cards on page 72 twice for each pair of players.
2. Have children color the game board and cards. Help children mount the cards on oaktag and cut out.
3. Glue the game board to the inside of a letter-sized file folder.
4. Glue the instructions to the front of the folder. Laminate.

BUILD AN IGLOO FILE-FOLDER GAME

HOW TO PLAY
(for 2 players)

1. Each player chooses an igloo. Two sets of playing cards (24 cards) are shuffled together and placed facedown in a pile.
2. Players take turns according to whose birthday comes earlier in the year. The first player draws one card from the deck, turns it over, and names the object shown on the card.
3. If the first letter of the object's name matches a letter on the player's igloo, the player covers the igloo letter with the card. If the name of the object does not match a letter on the igloo, the card is returned to the bottom of the deck.
4. The second player follows the same procedure.
5. Players continue to alternate drawing cards. If a player draws a card that he or she has already drawn earlier, the card is returned to the bottom of the deck.
6. Play continues until one player has covered all three ice blocks going across, down, or diagonally, as in "Bingo." That player is the winner.

Build an Igloo Game Card Patterns

COUNTING CARDS

Children can practice both addition and categorization skills with the following activity.

1. Pair each child with a partner. Give each child a set of 12 game cards from page 72.
2. Tell children to shuffle their cards and then lay out 6 in front of them, faceup, so their partner can see them.
3. Ask children:
   a) How many clothing items are there in all?
   b) How many animals are there in all?
   c) How many other items are there in all?
4. Have children collect their cards, shuffle them again, and repeat the procedure.
5. As a variation, each child may lay out more than or less than 6 cards, such as 4 cards, 7 cards, or 9 cards. After the cards have been laid out, ask the same three questions about the items.

WINTER WEATHER WHEEL

You need:
- crayons or markers
- scissors
- oaktag
- brass fastener
- glue

1. Reproduce the winter weather patterns on pages 75 through 77 once. Color and cut out.
2. Draw two circles each 36" in diameter on oaktag and cut out.
3. On one of the oaktag circles, arrange the five weather symbols, as shown.
4. Cut a large wedge out of the second oaktag circle, as shown.
5. Place the second circle on top of the first circle. Poke a hole through the center of each circle and attach with a brass fastener, as shown.
6. Glue the weather wheel decoration to the top circle.
7. Each day, ask volunteers to report on the weather conditions. Choose one child to turn the weather wheel to the appropriate weather symbol for the day. If two symbols are appropriate (for example, wind and rain), ask the class to choose which weather condition they consider to be stronger.

Winter Weather Patterns

WEATHER WHEEL

Winter Weather Patterns

THE NORTH WIND AND THE SUN—A FABLE

Read the story below to the class. Then discuss the moral of the story.

Once upon a time, the North Wind and the Sun were having an argument about which one was the stronger of the two.

"Oooooohhh!" bellowed the North Wind. "I am the strongest force in the world. People shiver and shake when they feel me!"

The Sun just smiled.

"Let's have a contest," suggested the North Wind. "Look at that little man down there walking, wearing a heavy coat. I'll make his coat come off. Just watch!"

The Sun just smiled.

The North Wind took a deep breath. He blew and blew. Cold and wintry wind howled everywhere all around the man. But the man only pulled his coat tightly around himself.

The North Wind grew angry. He blew even harder this time. But the man only pulled the coat around himself even more tightly.

The Sun just smiled.

"Oooooooohhh!" said the North Wind to the Sun. "So you think you can do better than me? Let's see you make that man's coat come off!"

The Sun began to smile even more brightly than before. Rays of warmth began to reach the man walking below. The Sun shined brighter and brighter, until finally the man stopped walking and took off his coat.

"How did you do that?" the North Wind demanded.

But the Sun just smiled.

Moral: Sometimes gentle persuasion works better than harsh treatment.

THE NORTH WIND AND THE SUN CLASS PLAY

You need:
• crayons or markers
• scissors
• hole puncher
• yarn
• coat

1. Reproduce the wind pattern on page 75 and the sun pattern on page 76 once. Color and cut out.
2. Punch a hole through the top of each figure. Then thread a length of yarn through each hole and tie together to make a necklace, as shown.
3. After reading the story of "The North Wind and the Sun" to the class, choose three children to act out the story. Have one child wear the North Wind necklace, one child wear the Sun necklace, and one child wear a coat and be the man below.
4. Encourage children to retell the story using their own words and actions. Let the entire class accompany the three children acting out the story by blowing when the North Wind blows, shivering when the man shivers, and so on. Repeat with different groups of three children for as long as interest allows.

WEATHER CHART

You need:
• crayons or markers
• scissors
• large piece of oaktag
• glue

1. Reproduce the weather symbols on pages 75 through 77 once. Color and cut out.
2. Using a large piece of oaktag, glue the weather symbols down the left side, as shown.
3. Draw a grid next to the weather symbols, as shown. Display the chart on a wall or bulletin board within children's reach.
4. After the weather conditions of the day have been discussed, choose one child to color in a square next to the appropriate weather symbol.
5. At the end of each week, have children count how many days have been sunny, rainy, windy, and so on. Have a class discussion about the weather for the week, and ask children what they think the weather might be for the upcoming week (for example, warmer or colder).

RECOMMENDED READING

Read some of the following books about winter weather to your class. Place the books on a reading table or in a bookcase so that children may look at them during free time.

Katy and the Big Snow by Virginia Lee Burton, published by Houghton Mifflin.
White Snow, Bright Snow by Alvin Tresselt, published by William Morrow.
The Day Daddy Stayed Home by Ethel and Leonard Kessler, published by Houghton Mifflin.
The Big Snow by Berta and Elmer Hader, published by Macmillan.
Owl Moon by Jane Yolen, published by Putnam.
The Snowy Day by Ezra Jack Keats, published by Penguin.